LET'S PLAY SPORTS!

Volleyball

by Kieran Downs

BLASTOFF!
2
READERS

BELLWETHER MEDIA • MINNEAPOLIS, MN

Blastoff! Readers are carefully developed by literacy experts to build reading stamina and move students toward fluency by combining standards-based content with developmentally appropriate text.

Level 1 provides the most support through repetition of high-frequency words, light text, predictable sentence patterns, and strong visual support.

Level 2 offers early readers a bit more challenge through varied sentences, increased text load, and text-supportive special features.

Level 3 advances early-fluent readers toward fluency through increased text load, less reliance on photos, advancing concepts, longer sentences, and more complex special features.

★ **Blastoff! Universe**

Reading Level

Blastoff! Beginners — Grade **K**

Blastoff! Readers — Grades **1–3**

Blastoff! Discovery — Grade **4**

This edition first published in 2021 by Bellwether Media, Inc.

No part of this publication may be reproduced in whole or in part without written permission of the publisher. For information regarding permission, write to Bellwether Media, Inc., Attention: Permissions Department, 6012 Blue Circle Drive, Minnetonka, MN 55343.

Library of Congress Cataloging-in-Publication Data

Names: Downs, Kieran, author.
Title: Volleyball / by Kieran Downs.
Description: Minneapolis, MN : Bellwether Media Inc., 2021. | Series: Blastoff! readers. Let's play sports! | Includes bibliographical references and index. | Audience: Ages 5-8 | Audience: Grades K-1 | Summary: "Relevant images match informative text in this introduction to volleyball. Intended for students in kindergarten through third grade"– Provided by publisher.
Identifiers: LCCN 2020029181 (print) | LCCN 2020029182 (ebook) | ISBN 9781644874288 (library binding) | ISBN 9781648341052 (ebook)
Subjects: LCSH: Volleyball–Juvenile literature.
Classification: LCC GV1015.34 .D69 2021 (print) | LCC GV1015.34 (ebook) | DDC 796.325–dc23
LC record available at https://lccn.loc.gov/2020029181
LC ebook record available at https://lccn.loc.gov/2020029182

Editor: Rebecca Sabelko   Designer: Josh Brink

Printed in the United States of America, North Mankato, MN.

Table of Contents

What Is Volleyball?

Volleyball is a team sport played on a **court**.

Players use their arms and hands to hit a ball over a net. Teams try to score the most points!

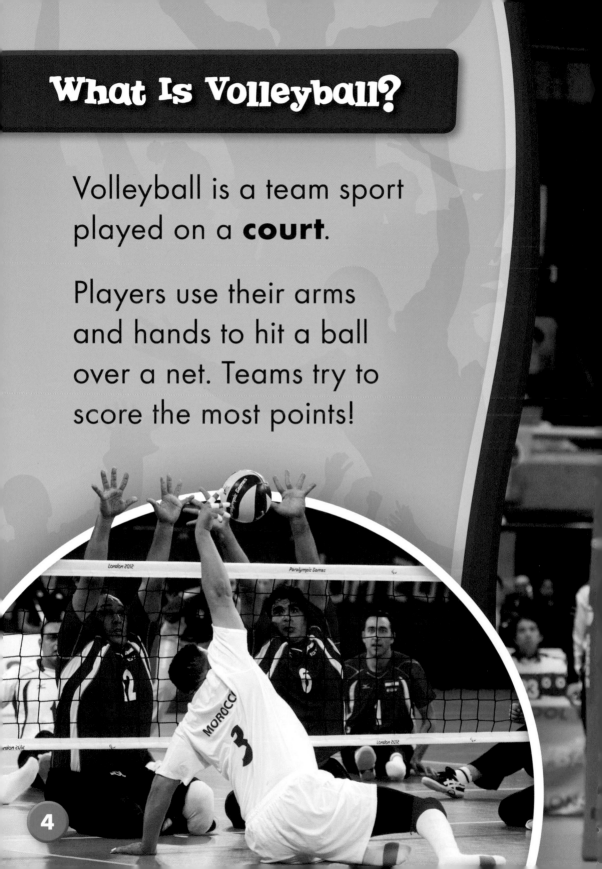

net

Volleyball became a sport in 1895. It was added to the **Olympic Games** in 1964. Russia holds the most volleyball Olympic medals.

2016 Summer Olympics in Brazil

Jordan Larson

- United States Women's Volleyball Team

- Outside Hitter

- Accomplishments:
  - Captain of the United States Women's Volleyball Team
  - 2012 Olympic Games team silver medal
  - 2016 Olympic Games team bronze medal
  - 2015 and 2016 USA Volleyball Female Indoor Player of the Year

The sport is popular around the world.

What Are the Rules for Volleyball?

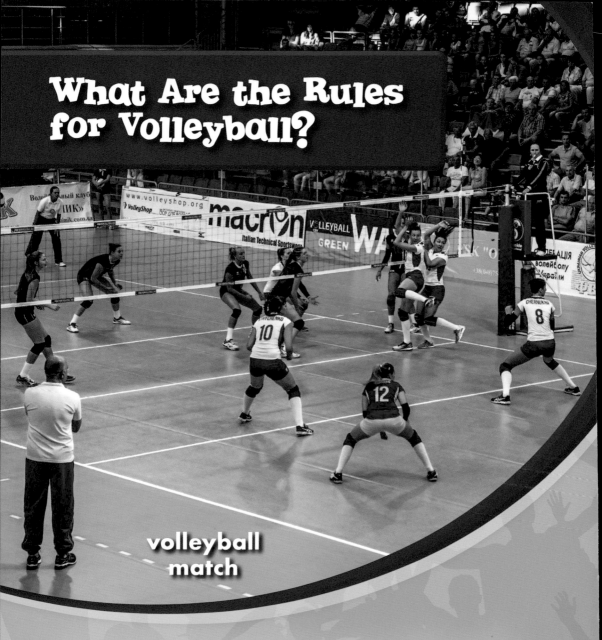

volleyball match

Volleyball **matches** are played in **sets**. Most sets go up to 25 points. They must be won by 2 or more points.

The team that wins the
most sets wins the match!

Six players from each team play at one time.

Play begins when a player **serves** the ball over the net.

serve

11

Each team can hit the ball three times. The **libero** bumps the ball.

libero

going for a spike

The **setter** puts it into position.
The **attacker** goes for a **spike**!

blockers

A **blocker** on the other team
tries to stop the attack.

If the ball is not blocked, a **passer** is ready to **dig** the ball.

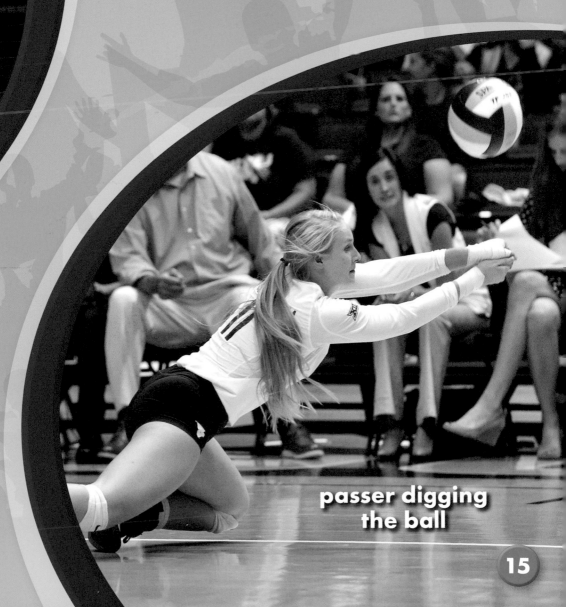

passer digging the ball

Teams earn a point when the other team cannot return the ball.

missing a return

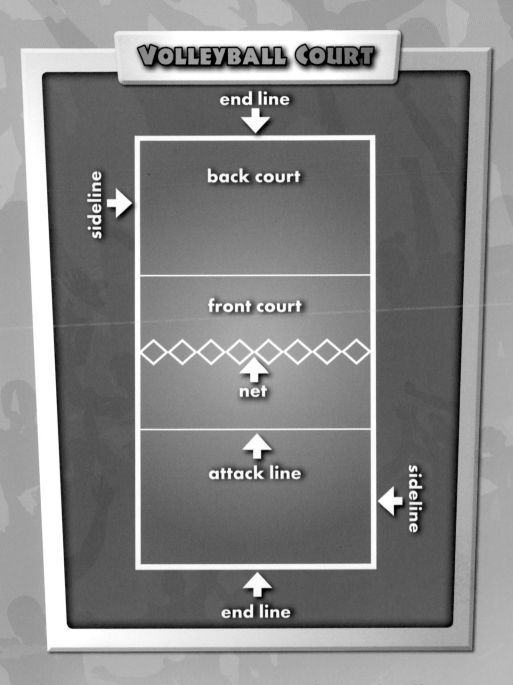

VOLLEYBALL COURT

end line

back court

sideline

front court

net

attack line

sideline

end line

They also score if the ball
goes **out of bounds**.

knee pads

Volleyball players wear lightweight clothes. These allow them to make quick moves.

Volleyball Gear

net

volleyball

shoes

lightweight clothes

Knee pads keep their knees safe when they dive. Special shoes help players move easily.

Volleyball nets are over
7 feet (2 meters) tall.
The net goes across the
whole court.

Go for a spike!

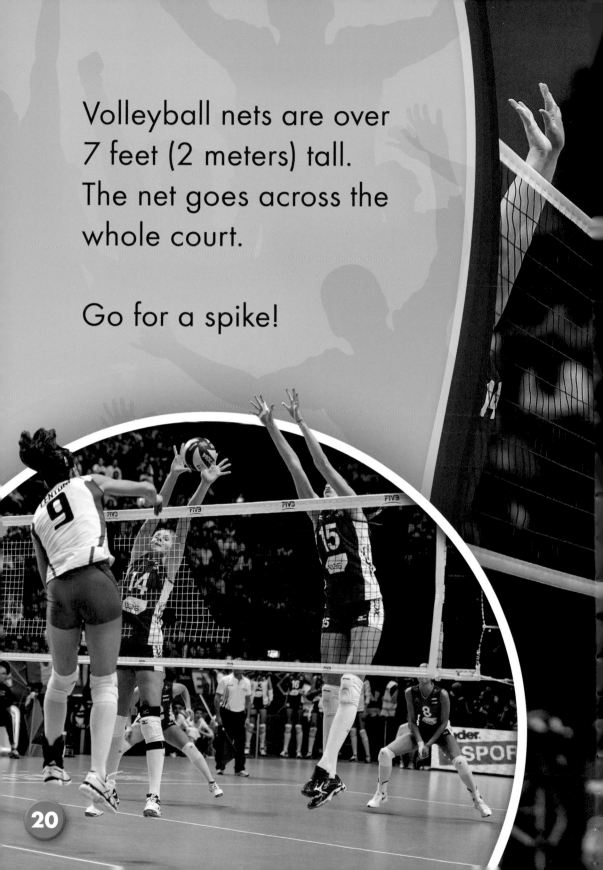

Glossary

attacker—a player who plays in the front of the court and tries to score points; attackers are also called spikers or hitters.

blocker—a player who plays along the net and blocks the other team's attacks

court—the area that volleyball is played on

dig—to pass a spiked ball

libero—a player who always plays in the back row and specializes in passing off serves; the libero wears a different colored jersey.

matches—contests between two or more individuals or teams

Olympic Games—worldwide summer or winter sports contests held in a different country every four years

out of bounds—outside the area in which a game is played

passer—a player who digs or bumps hits made by the other team

serves—hits the ball to start play

sets—groups of games that count towards deciding a winner; most volleyball matches have three or five sets.

setter—a player who sets up the ball for attackers to hit

spike—a downward hit over the net that tries to score a point; spikes are also called hits or attacks.

To Learn More

Doeden, Matt. *Volleyball*. Mankato, Minn.: Amicus High Interest, 2016.

Donner, Erica. *Volleyball*. Minneapolis, Minn.: Jump!, 2017.

Fretland VanVoorst, Jenny. *The Science Behind Volleyball*. Minneapolis, Minn.: Jump!, 2020.

ON THE WEB

FACTSURFER

Factsurfer.com gives you a safe, fun way to find more information.

1. Go to www.factsurfer.com.

2. Enter "volleyball" into the search box and click 🔍.

3. Select your book cover to see a list of related content.

Index

The images in this book are reproduced through the courtesy of: David Davis Photoproductions RF/ Alamy, front cover (hero); Pavel L Photo and Video, front cover (background), p. 19 (bottom right); Bob Daemmrich/ Alamy, p. 4; Aflo Co. Ltd./ Alamy, pp. 4-5, 7; Alexander Vilf/ AP Images, p. 6; A-Lesik, pp. 8, 9, 11; Timothy Mulholland/ Alamy, p. 10; Ettore Griffoni, p. 12; Celso Pupo, pp. 13, 14; Aspenphoto, p. 15, Alexander Mitrofanov/ Alamy, p. 16; FatCamera, pp. 18-19; David Lee, p. 19 (top left); Ivanhoe Koubek, p. 19 (top right); Eugene Onischenko, p. 19 (bottom left); Paolo Bona, p. 20; JoeSAPhotos, pp. 20-21; Milos Kontic, p. 23.